ILLUSTRATED SKIING DICTIONARY FOR YOUNG PEOPLE

BY CLAIRE WALTER

ILLUSTRATED BY

MICHAEL SNYDER

HARVEY HOUSE, Publishers
New York, New York

HARVEY HOUSE, Publishers
20 Waterside Plaza, New York, New York 10010

FOREWORD

Skiing was developed thousands of years ago by people living in the far north of Europe and Asia. They fashioned primitive skis to help them travel over snow during long winters.

Skiing for pleasure developed in Scandinavia early in the 1800s. Towns soon put on colorful winter carnivals, which often included both cross-country and jumping contests. As people skied for fun, techniques evolved for turning, stopping and steering, but cross-country and jumping remained the two main branches of what has come to be called Nordic skiing.

Nordic Skiing

Cross-country skiing is the national sport of the Scandinavian countries. There children learn how to ski almost as soon as they can walk. For many years it was eclipsed in America by the popularity of flashy downhill skiing. But in the late 1960s a boom in recreational cross-country skiing began and is still going on. Today, cross-country rivals downhill in popularity.

Ski jumping is a sport most Scandinavian boys begin when they are still quite small. In the United States where there aren't many jumping hills, there are not too many oppor-

1

tunities to learn and practice the sport. Nevertheless, people who have learned to ski jump say it is thrilling — as close as humans come to unaided flight.

Alpine Skiing

Skiing was introduced to the rugged mountains of Australia, Canada and the United States in the middle of the nineteenth century. An American mail carrier named John A. "Snowshoe" Thompson became legendary by maintaining the only contact between the eastern states and California through the winter of 1856 by skiing over the High Sierra range.

In the late nineteenth century, the people of Central Europe began importing skis from Scandinavia and adapting ski techniques to the steep mountainsides of the Alps. There were no ski lifts yet, and skiers had to hike up to be able to ski down.

The greatest innovator in Alpine skiing, as this branch of the sport became known, was an Austrian named Hannes Schneider. In the 1920s, he invented a systemized method for teaching skiing. His Arlberg Technique consisted of a progression that started with the snowplow and continued through snowplow turn, stem turn and stem christie until the pupil was ready to master the parallel turn. Schneider taught instructors this progression, and the Arlberg Technique remained the standard for Alpine skiing for decades.

All this time, skis were long, heavy wood boards. It was considered quite an achievement when metal edges were developed that could be screwed onto wooden skis. Old-time boots, which looked much like today's hiking boots, were made of leather and laced up. The boots were affixed to the skis by bindings which consisted of metal clamps and long leather straps.

There was some recreational skiing in the United States before World War II, but it was not as well developed as in Europe where there were many resorts and ski schools all over the Alps. After the war, skiing boomed in America. Hannes Schneider had come to New Hampshire, bringing his Arlberg Technique across the Atlantic to a country ready to learn how to ski.

Beginning late in the 1950s, wooden skis gave way to metal and finally fiberglass models. Lace boots were replaced by buckle boots, and plastic took the place of leather. Release bindings were invented to make skiing safer. With each such advance, skiing became easier. Also, ski areas in America began grooming their slopes and learning to make snow.

Innovations included new ways of teaching beginners how to ski. American ski schools pioneered ways of having beginners learn on very short, easy-to-turn skis, and soon new skiers were able to avoid the long, tedious exercises of the Arlberg Technique.

Competition

It seems to be human nature that wherever there is a recreational sport, people like to compete to see who is best at it. The first important Nordic championship, an outgrowth of the old Scandinavian town carnivals, was held in 1892. It was called the *Holmenkollen,* which is Norwegian for "king's crown," and it is still the most important annual competition for the world's best cross-country racers and ski jumpers.

The major Alpine races attracting elite skiers were begun between the two World Wars: the Arlberg-Kandahar in 1928, the Lauberhorn in 1930 and the Hahnenkamm in 1933. Like the Holmenkollen for Nordic skiers, these races are still the most important for Alpine racers.

The major international races have been combined into organized circuits known as the "World Cup." The best Alpine and Nordic competitors travel from place to place throughout the winter to compete for points. At the end of each winter, the best men and women receive prizes for season-long excellence in their sport. The Alpine World Cup was founded in 1967, and the Nordic World Cup came into being 12 years later. Top World Cup racers are as well known in Europe as baseball or tennis stars are in North America.

Still, the most coveted single honor in skiing is an Olympic gold medal. Ski jumping and men's cross-country events were included in the very first Winter Olympics in 1924. Alpine races for both men and women were added in 1936. Cross-country races for women were not included until 1964. Biathlon, a little-known men's sport that consists of cross-country and rifle marksmanship developed from Scandinavian military training, became an olympic sport in 1960.

Today there are six Olympic Alpine events: slalom, giant slalom and downhill for men and women. Nordic events include five-kilometer, ten-kilometer and relay cross-country for women; and 15-kilometer, 30-kilometer, 50-kilometer and relay races, 70- and 90-meter ski jumping and Nordic combined for men. There are also individual and relay biathlon competitions.

Although world-class competitors are heavily subsidized, these athletes are called "amateurs." Professional ski racing, where skiers compete openly for prize money, was a dream for many years. In the 1960s former

U.S. Ski Team coach Bob Beattie founded a professional racing circuit for men. While amateurs ski one at a time against the clock, pro racing developed a format pitting two racers against one another on parallel courses. This head-to-head racing is exciting to watch. Leading men now earn tens of thousands of dollars a year, and a successful women's pro circuit has come along too.

Freestyle skiing, on the other hand, began as a professional sport in the early 1970s. Freestylers burst onto the skiing scene, bringing to the slopes such showy elements as ballet-like routines and acrobatic stunts performed in midair. Freestylers received much attention and the best of them earned a great deal of money. A series of severe injuries in aerial competition curtailed professional freestyle meets in just a few years. Nevertheless, amateur freestyle is still popular among young skiers, who hope it will someday be an Olympic sport.

Ski competition begins on a club or local level for youngsters of kindergarten age with short races that are more fun than serious. Before skiers are ten, however, they can begin competing with racers from other clubs. The United States Ski Association and its divisions have many competitions for Alpine and Nordic skiers of all age groups. By the time they are in their early teens, the best racers

compete against skiers from all over the
United States, and the best of these are
eventually invited to join the U.S. Ski Team.
U.S.S.T. skiers in turn compete against the
best in the world. Canada and other countries
have similar systems of putting together a
national team.

Recreational Skiing

For most people, skiing is just pleasurable winter recreation. There are nearly a thousand lift-served ski areas in the United States and Canada for Alpine skiing, and hundreds more in Europe and elsewhere in the world. There are also several hundred ski-touring centers and countless miles of hiking trails, golf courses and untracked routes in meadows and mountains for cross-country.

Alpine skis are usually about as high as a skier's head. Boots are made of rigid plastic and are affixed to the skis by release bindings. Cross-country skis are much narrower and lighter in weight. The binding attaches the boot sole to the ski only at the toe. The heel is left free so that the foot can flex during the striding motion. Cross-country boots are low-cut lace shoes which look like running shoes that have a slightly protruding sole for hooking the binding on. Poles for both are strong and light in weight.

Skiing can be an exciting international sporting event or a very personal way of getting into the fresh air and enjoying winter. The sport has its own vocabulary to describe both the competitive and recreational aspects of skiing.

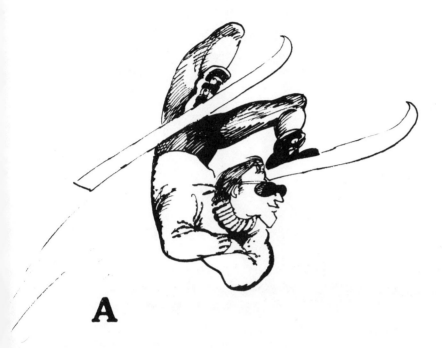

A

Aerials — freestyle skiing maneuvers done in the air after the skier has taken off from a ramp-like hump of snow. *(See Freestyle.)*

Alpine combined — a competition that is determined by a skier's combined performance in downhill and slalom.

Alpine skiing — skiing downhill on a mountain. In racing, Alpine skiing is comprised of three disciplines: slalom, giant slalom and downhill. Alpine skiing began in the Alps of Central Europe.

Angulation — the body position in which the knees and hips are rolled toward the hill in order to edge the skis while the upper body is angled outward for balance.

Anorak — the European word for *parka*. (See *Parka*.)

Anticipation — pivoting the body slightly in the direction required for the next turn.

Antifriction device — a small Teflon pad or sliding mechanical device mounted on the ski under the ball of the foot to aid binding release by reducing friction between boot and ski.

Arlberg Kandahar — one of the most prestigious international Alpine World Cup races which rotates annually among four European ski resorts. They are: St. Anton, Austria; Murren, Switzerland; Garmisch, West Germany; Chamonix, France.

Arlberg Technique — a progression of ski intruction developed in Austria in the 1930s. It became the most common form of learning for several decades. It was characterized by extreme rotation of the entire body. It has since been replaced by newer methods. (See *A.T.M.*)

A-Team — the top-ranked group of skiers of a ski team.

A.T.M. — American Teaching Method, the ski instruction progression developed by the Professional Ski Instructors of America. This method starts the beginner on very short skis, gradually increasing the skis' length as the pupil becomes comfortable.

Attack — racing term to describe aggressive technique on the course.

Avalanche — a mass of snow that slides down the side of a mountain. A rare but very dangerous occurence at ski resorts.

B

Baby hill — nickname for a beginners' slope.

Baby lift — nickname for a lift, often a rope tow, on a beginners' slope.

Ballet — freestyle skiing maneuvers done on a smooth, flat slope choreographed into a routine and set to music. Ballet consists of such tricks as turns, changes of directon, one-foot skiing and acrobatics.

Basket — a perforated disc of metal or plastic affixed several inches from the tip of a ski pole to prevent the pole from being pushed too deep into the snow.

Beartrap — nickname for an old-fashioned metal and leather binding, no longer in use, in which the boot is clamped to the ski.

Bench testing — evaluating skis by measuring dimensions, torsion, flex and other technical properties, when there are no boots affixed to them.

Biathlon — a competition which combines cross-country racing and rifle shooting. The score is determined by a combination of elapsed time and accuracy in hitting targets along the course.

Binding — the mechanical device which fastens the boot to the ski. (See *Beartrap, Cable binding, Release binding.*)

Binding check — a mechanical test to check the release capability of a binding.

Blue ice — an extremely icy condition caused by water freezing directly over rock.

Boilerplate — an icy snow condition caused by snow which has partially melted and refrozen.

Bottom filing — running a file across the bottom of a ski to remove concave or convex unevenness.

Bowl — a large semicircular portion of a mountain which is considered to be very desirable ski terrain.

Brown bag — bringing one's own lunch to eat at a ski area.

B-Team — the second-ranked group of skiers
on a team.

Bumps — in professional racing, large bumps of snow built into slalom and giant slalom courses to add challenge to the race.

Bump skiing — another name for *mogul skiing.*

Bunny — nickname for a beginning skier.

Bunny hill — nickname for a beginners' slope.

C

Cable binding — a binding in which the toe of the boot is held firmly against the binding toepiece by a cable around the heel. Today, cable bindings are used only in ski mountaineering.

Camber — an arc built into the ski to help distribute the skier's weight along its full length. When a ski is placed on a flat surface and no weight is applied to it, only the tip and tail touch the surface.

Can-Am Series — a circuit of Alpine races held in the United States and Canada for competitors ranking below World Cup levels.

Canting — building up or shaving down a boot sole or inserting a wedge under one side of the binding to distribute the skier's weight evenly across the ski.

Carving — the action of setting the ski on edge in order to turn with a minimum of skidding or sideslipping.

24

Catching an edge — stumbling when an edge hooks into the snow causing the skier to be thrown off balance or to fall.

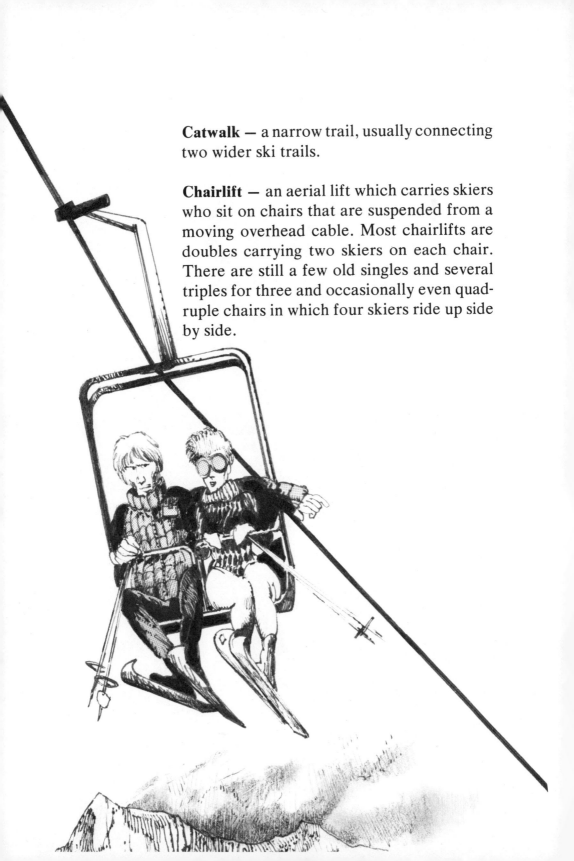

Catwalk — a narrow trail, usually connecting two wider ski trails.

Chairlift — an aerial lift which carries skiers who sit on chairs that are suspended from a moving overhead cable. Most chairlifts are doubles carrying two skiers on each chair. There are still a few old singles and several triples for three and occasionally even quadruple chairs in which four skiers ride up side by side.

Chatter — the vibration caused by skiing over extremely rough terrain.

Check — a maneuver used to slow down skis, usually accomplished by thrusting one or both skis slightly to one side.

Christie — a turn in which the skis are parallel to each other as the turn is completed.

Citizen's racing — ski races such as NAS TAR, family races, ski-club challenge races and others which may be entered by the general public, usually by paying a small entry fee.

Climbing skins — strips of sealskin or synthetic fabric affixed temporarily to the bottoms of skis to assist in climbing without slideback. Today, skins are used only in ski mountaineering.

Closed gate — a slalom gate in which the two poles are set vertically on the hill, requiring the racer to ski across the fall line.

Comma position — a term formerly used to describe extreme angulation.

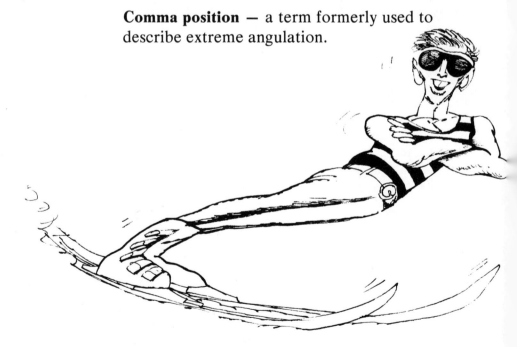

Control gate — a set of double slalom poles, linked by a flag, marking the safest line through dangerous sections of a downhill course. Racers who fail to pass through each control gate are disqualified.

Corn — a snow condition associated with spring skiing in which the snow forms large, loosely packed granules which resemble corn off the cob.

Cornice — a ledge of snow or ice.

Counter-rotation — any turn in which the motion of the body around an imaginary axis is made in the opposite direction from the turn.

Course inspection — in giant slalom and slalom, the racers climb up beside the course to study it and memorize the combinations of gates. Only in downhill are practice runs permitted on the actual course before a race. (See *Nonstop.*)

Course markers — small flags or evergreen branches used to mark the outer edges of a downhill racing course.

Criterium of the First Snow — the first Alpine World Cup race of the season, held at Val d'Isère, France.

Critical point — see *K-point*.

Cross-country — skiing generally on flat open areas, as opposed to down mountainsides. This involves skiing across flats, climbing hills and sliding down. The skis are powered by strong leg motions, rather than using a slope to gain speed.

Crossed skis — two crossed skis stuck into the snow signal that an injured skier is lying on the slope below.

Crossing tips — overlapping the tips while skiing, which frequently causes a loss of balance or a fall.

Crossover — a ballet trick in which the skier steps one ski across the other.

Crud — a snow condition consisting of softer snow topped by a thin breakable crust.

C.S.I.A. — Canadian Ski Instructors' Alliance, the association of professional ski instructors in Canada.

C-Team — the third-ranked skiers on a team. These are usually young, up-and-coming racers in the early stages of their competitive careers.

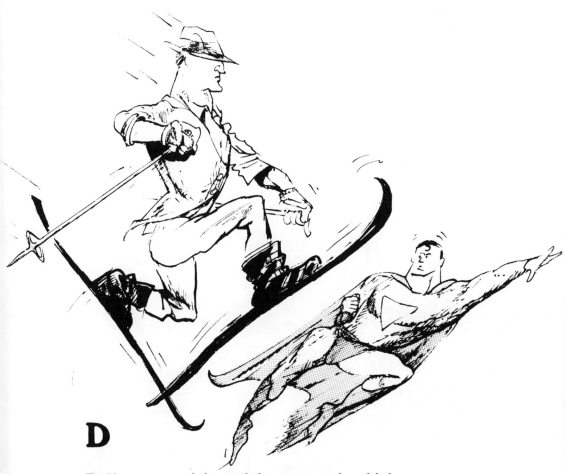

D

Daffy — an upright aerial maneuver in which the skier imitates the motion of walking in the air. Two "steps" constitute a single daffy; four steps make a double.

Demo skis — demonstration model skis which are sometimes lent to potential customers by ski shops or manufacturers' ski representatives.

Diagonal stride — the basic technique of cross-country skiing, which is essentially a walking stride. The left foot and right arm and the right foot and the left arm move forward in pairs. The diagonal stride consists of the kick and glide.

Direct-to-parallel — an approach to ski instruction in which beginners are taught a rough, wide-track parallel turn which they refine as their ski ability improves. (See *Wide-track turn.*)

Double poling — the cross-country maneuver of poling with both arms simultaneously with or without the kick, usually done on a flat or by racers to gain speed.

Downhill — the discipline of Alpine ski racing which requires one run down a long course consisting of bumps, dropoffs, gulleys and flats. Racers attain the highest speeds in downhill. In World Cup racing, competitors are often clocked at more than 80 miles an hour on the fastest parts of the course. A World Cup downhill course may be up to two miles long and have a vertical drop of up to 3,200 for men and 2,300 feet for women.

Downhill ski — in a traverse, the ski which is lower on the slope.

Downhill suit — a tight-fitting, one-piece suit worn by downhill racers to cut down on wind resistance.

Drag — using the poles to help slow down on a downhill portion of a cross-country course. When approaching such a downhill, the skier removes the pole straps from the wrists, puts the skis in a snowplow position, angles the poles between the legs pointing well to the back to act as a brake and applies body pressure onto the dragging poles. Also called "pole drag."

Drag lift — the British term for surface lift.

Dry-land training — exercises performed by racers to strengthen specific muscles required for skiing and increased agility.

E

Edge — a strip of metal inserted into each side of the ski-bottom surface to protect it and allow the ski, when properly sharpened, to hold on icy or very hard snow.

Edge set — increasing the holding action of the skis by rolling the body weight to dig the edges more firmly into the snow.

Edging — controlling sideslip by setting the skis' edges into the snow. (See *Sideslip.*)

Eggbeater — a windmilling fall in which a skier —with skis still attached — rolls and tumbles a substantial distance down the hill. This occurs mostly in downhill racing, because skiers attain high speeds and bindings have been tightened to avoid accidental release while skiing.

Egg position — in downhill racing, a version of the tuck, in which the back is slightly rounded, knees bent, arms held against body. The egg position is used when the racer wants to go as fast as possible.

Elbow — a combination of one closed slalom gate followed directly below by an open gate.

Europa Cup — an international circuit of Alpine races held in Europe for competitors ranking just below those on the World Cup tour, after which it is patterned.

Exhibition skiing — an early name for "freestyle."

F

Face — the steepest part of a mountain.

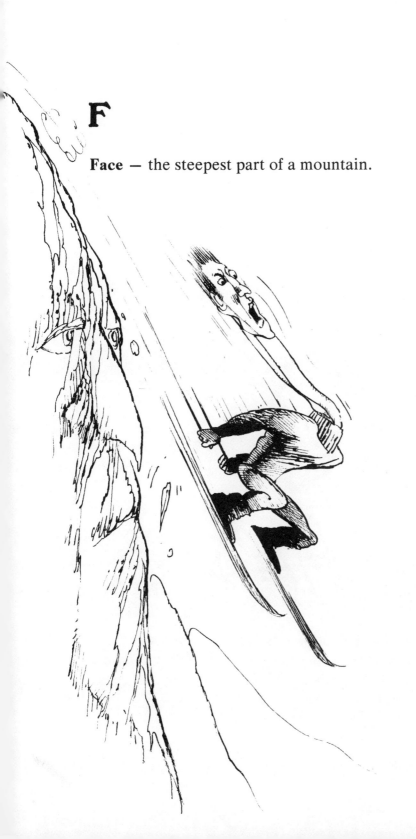

Fall line — the shortest line down the hill, the line a ball would roll down if released down the hill.

Fanny pack — a small pack worn on a belt around the hips to carry ski paraphernalia or, by ski patrollers, for first-aid equipment.

Fiberglass skis — skis whose main structural element is fiberglass. Today, fiberglass is used for virtually all Alpine skis and most cross-country skis.

Finish line — the final gate at the end of a race course which contains electronic timing equipment to determine elapsed time for each skier's run.

F.I.S. — *Fédération Internationale de Ski,* the international governing body for Alpine and Nordic ski competition.

Fishscale — a type of ski bottom made of overlapping semicircles of plastic. Now used primarily for touring skis, the fishscale base is designed so that the ski can slide forward but not slip backward.

Flex — a ski's ability to bend. A ski which bends easily is described as having a soft flex; one which is resistant to bending is described as being stiff.

Flow boot — a ski boot whose lining is made of a flexible material that will mold itself slowly around the foot of the wearer.

Flush — a series of three closed slalom gates, set one below the other, requiring the racer to make two quick turns to ski the combination.

Foam boot — a ski boot whose lining is poured or injected around the foot while the buyer is wearing it to produce a custom fit.

Forerunner — a skier who makes a run down a race course before the competitors start to help officials evaluate course conditions. It is considered an honor to be invited to forerun a race course.

BUT...

Four-event skier — a skier who competes in cross-country, ski jumping, slalom and giant slalom. (See *Skimeister.*)

Free skiing — a term used by racers to describe skiing other than race training and racing.

Freestyle — an overall term designating ski competition which developed in the early 1970s. Freestyle, which is judged on a point system by a panel of judges, has various elements: aerial, ballet and mogul.

Funicular — a type of lift, fairly common in Europe, which consists of two sets of enclosed cars which ride on cables over tracks. One set of cars goes up while the other set comes down. Riders generally stand up in the cars.

44

G

Gaiters — elasticized cuffs of waterproof fabric which some skiers put over their boot tops to prevent snow from seeping in.

Garland — a series of turns in the same direction, such as a series of uphill christies, which can be used to control speed.

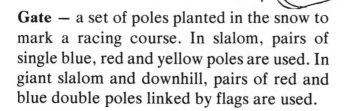

Gate — a set of poles planted in the snow to mark a racing course. In slalom, pairs of single blue, red and yellow poles are used. In giant slalom and downhill, pairs of red and blue double poles linked by flags are used.

HERE T'IS!

Gatekeeper — an official stationed along a race course to monitor the racers' passage through each gate and to reset poles knocked down by competitors.

Gelandy — a jump on Alpine skis made off a bump in an attempt to travel as far as possible before landing. Gelandy is the Americanized abbreviation for the German term, *Geländesprung.*

Geschmozzle start — nickname for old-fashioned mass-start Alpine races. (See *Mass start.)*

Giant slalom — the discipline of Alpine ski racing which combines some of the characteristics of slalom and downhill. Run on a medium-length course, giant slalom requires almost the agility of slalom and the speed of downhill. The course is longer than a slalom but shorter than a downhill; the gates are farther apart than in slalom. The combined time of two runs determines a racer's results in a giant slalom race. A World Cup giant slalom race has about 30 gates.

Glade — a wooded section of a slope cleared of underbrush so that skiers can ski among the trees.

Glide — the sliding portion of the diagonal stride of cross-country skiing which is generated by the kick. The glide serves as a small pause for resting between kicks.

G.L.M. — Graduated Length Method, a system of ski instruction devised in the United States in the 1960s, in which beginning skiers started on extremely short skis and, as they progressed, "graduated" to longer skis. Many of the early principles of G.L.M. have now been incorporated into the American Teaching Method. (See *A.T.M., P.S.I.A.*)

Goggles — large lenses encased in a padded frame which fits close to the face to guard the eyes against bright sunshine, wind or snow. Usually, green lenses are worn in bright sunlight and yellow lenses are used on gray, overcast days.

Gondola — an aerial lift consisting of cabins suspended from a moving cable, typically for three to six skiers each. Riders remove their skis, which are carried in tubelike holders on the outside of each gondola car.

Groove — an indentation running along the bottom of a ski.

G. S. — abbreviation for giant slalom.

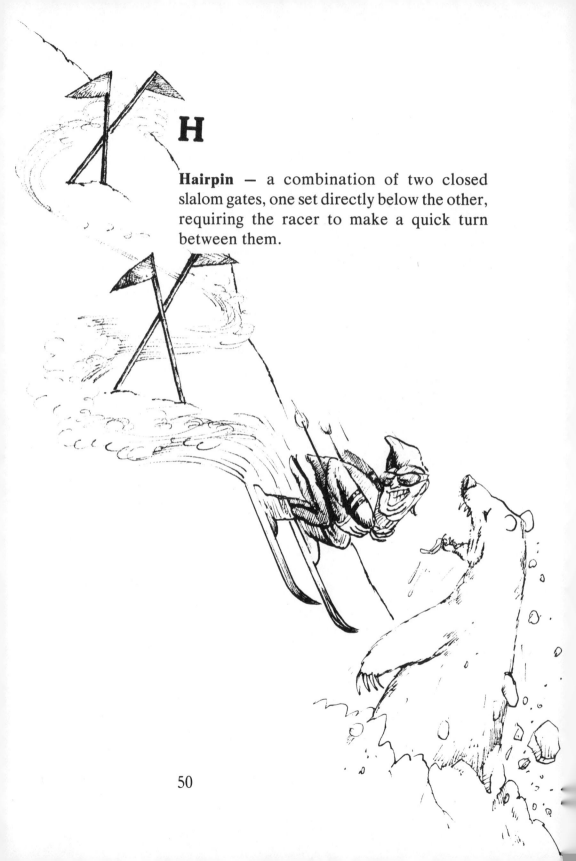

H

Hairpin — a combination of two closed slalom gates, one set directly below the other, requiring the racer to make a quick turn between them.

50

Hardpack — snow that has been packed down so that it forms an extremely firm skiing surface.

Hard wax — cross-country wax which comes in cake or stick form to be melted or rubbed onto the ski. There are gliding waxes which are used on the tip and tail, and kicking waxes are used under the foot. All brands include waxes in several colors to handle various snow temperatures. Green (for the coldest); blue, red and yellow (for the warmest snow) are offered by most wax manufacturers. Hard wax is used for new snow.

Head-to-head racing — slalom or giant slalom in which two racers compete at the same time on side-by-side courses set with identical gates. Also called "parallel racing."

Heelpiece — the portion of a binding which holds the heel of the boot to the ski.

Heelthrust — the act of pushing the tails of both skis off to one side as a method of checking speed. (See *check.*)

Helicopter — an upright aerial maneuver in which the skier does an upright, 360-degree turn between takeoff and landing.

Helicopter skiing — skiing in terrain not served by lifts but using helicopters for uphill transport.

Herringbone — a method of climbing a hill with the skis in a V position, with the tails together and the tips pointed outward in opposite directions.

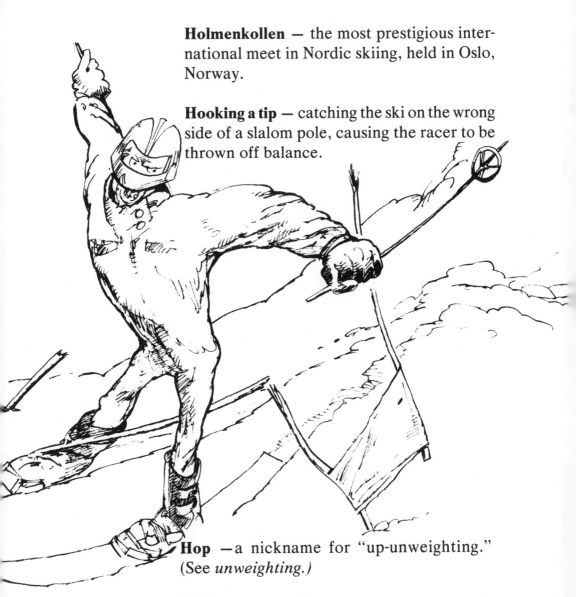

Holmenkollen — the most prestigious inter-national meet in Nordic skiing, held in Oslo, Norway.

Hooking a tip — catching the ski on the wrong side of a slalom pole, causing the racer to be thrown off balance.

Hop — a nickname for "up-unweighting." (See *unweighting.*)

Hotdog — the nickname for an extremely aggressive and showy skier.

Hotshot — an expert skier, usually used to describe a show-off.

Hot wax — wax which must be melted and ironed onto a ski bottom.

I

Inrun — the steep section of the ramp where a jumper picks up speed prior to takeoff.

Interval timing — the timing of racers over individual sections of a course. Also called "split timing," it gauges how well the racer is handling certain portions of the course.

Inverted aerials — maneuvers in freestyle skiing which include at least one head-over-heels, 360-degree revolution in the air. Many inverted aerials are similar to diving maneuvers. (See *Aerials, Freestyle.*)

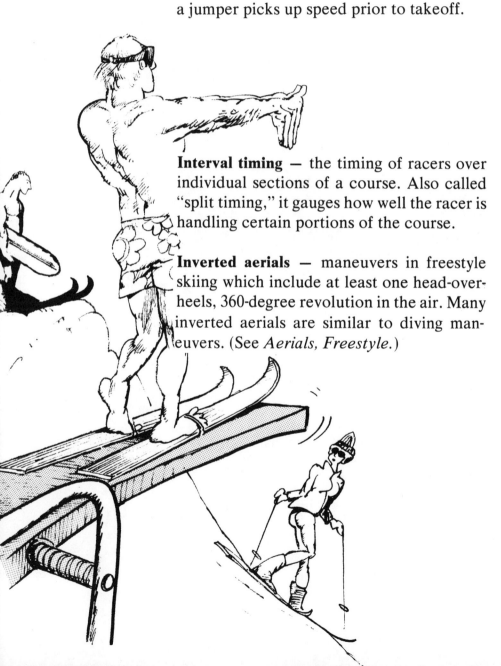

J

J-bar — a lift which pulls skiers uphill by a series of J-shaped poles suspended from a moving overhead cable. Each "J" carries one skier, who stands up propelled by the device and with skis remaining on the snow.

Jet turn — a high-speed turn done with down-unweighting motion during which the skis briefly shoot out ahead of the skier's body, giving him or her the appearance of being in a sitting position.

K

Kick — the portion of the cross-country diagonal stride which provides the propulsion to move the skier across the snow. The base construction of the ski or the wax provides the ability for the kick.

Kick turn — a technique for changing direction while standing still, especially useful for turning around at the edge of a steep slope. Standing perpendicular to the fall line, the skier first plants both poles above the uphill ski and balances lightly against them. Then, he or she lifts the downhill ski and rests it on the tail. Then the downhill ski is replaced on the snow in the opposite direction from the uphill ski. The maneuver is completed by lifting the poles and pivoting the uphill ski around the downhill ski.

Kilometro Lanciato — "The flying kilometer," a competition held each summer to determine the fastest speed attainable on skis. Using special superlong skis, the competitors schuss straight down a long, smooth drop. The *Kilometro Lanciato* has traditionally been held in Cervinia, Italy, but in the 1980s is expected to move to Portillo, Chile. Steve McKinney set a new record in 1979: 200.22 miles per hour!

Klister — a soft, paste-like cross-country wax which comes in a tube and is used for old snow or warm, wet snow.

Knickers — loose-fitting pants that end just below the knee and are worn with high socks. Knickers are popular for cross-country, although they were once common attire for Alpine skiers as well.

Knoll — the down-curving portion of the landing hill under the lip of a ski jump.

K-point — designation for the critical point of the landing hill below a ski jump — the middle of the flat transition section between the knoll and the outrun.

L

Langlauf — German word for cross-country skiing.

Latch-in binding — a binding which must be manually snapped shut when the skier has put his or her boot into it.

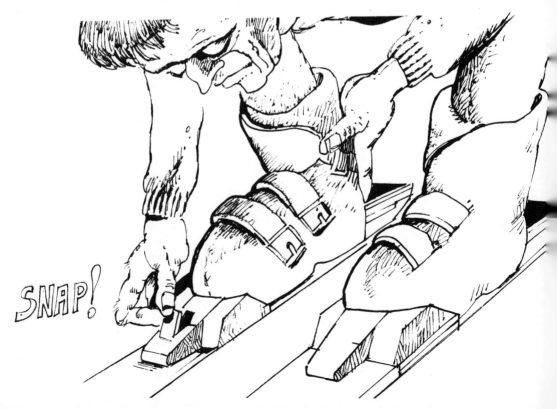

Liftline — the queue of skiers waiting to load onto a ski lift. Also, the cleared section under a lift.

Lift pass — a form of identification indicating that a skier has paid for use of the lifts for several days or even a season. Frequently, a lift pass includes the skier's photograph and is worn on a chain around the neck.

Lift ticket — a ticket, usually affixed to the skier's clothing by means of a short wire, which indicates that the person has paid to use the lift. In the United States, most ski areas sell tickets for all-day, half-day or night skiing.

Lift tower — a metal tower used to support the cables of a ski lift.

Line — the route skied, such as the path chosen through a mogul field or through slalom gates.

Linked turns — turns made one after another without a traverse between them. (See *traverse.)*

Lip — the edge of a jump, in ski jumping or freestyle aerials.

Loipe — German word for a cross-country track.

Longjohns — thermal underwear worn under ski clothing to insulate the skier from the cold. Longjohns come in two parts, tops and bottoms.

M

Machine made snow — snow manufactured by combining compressed air and water in subfreezing temperatures. Also called man-made snow and artificial snow. (See *Snow gun, Snowmaking.*)

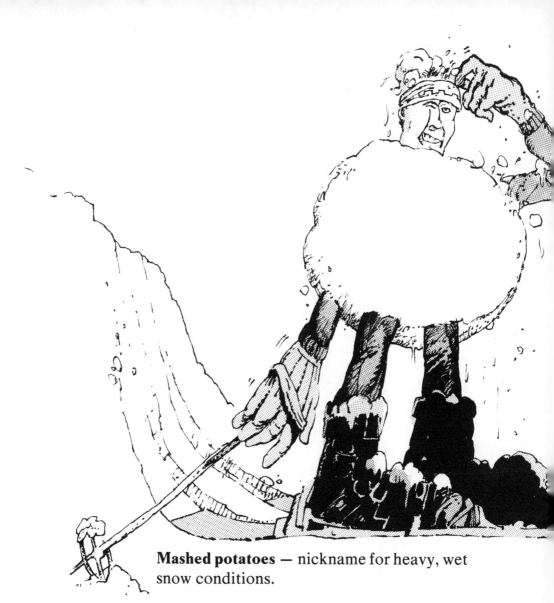

Mashed potatoes — nickname for heavy, wet snow conditions.

Mass start — beginning a race with all competitors massed at a starting line and taking off at the same time on the "go" command. This method is now used for cross-country races and was formerly used for some Alpine races too.

Metal skis — skis whose main structural element is metal, often around a wooden core. Metal skis were at their height of popularity for Alpine skiing in the 1960s.

Missing a gate — failure to ski between slalom poles of the same color during a race, which results in disqualification. A skier who has missed a gate may choose to climb back up to ski through the gate and continue to race. Knocking down a pole does not result in disqualification.

Mitey Mite — a brand name for a simple tow which consists of handles attached to a loop of moving rope. Skiers grab the handles and are towed uphill.

Moebius flip — in freestyle skiing, an inverted aerial maneuver consisting of a somersault with a full twist. When two somersaults and a twist are done, it is a double Moebius.

Mogul — a bump in the snow built up by many skiers' turns in the same place.

Mogul field — a slope, usually fairly steep, dotted with bumps of snow.

Mogul skiing — portion of freestyle which requires the skier to produce an exciting nonstop run down a steep, heavily moguled course.

Mule kick — an upright aerial maneuver in which the skier kicks both skis off to one side while in the air.

N

NASTAR — National Standard Ski Race, a giant slalom race designed for America's recreational skiers. Each skier's time is measured against a national standard, and a recreational racer coming within a certain percentage of the pacesetter's time is awarded a gold, silver or bronze medal. (See *Pacesetter.*)

Nations Cup — a trophy awarded to the national ski team accumulating the greatest number of Alpine World Cup points in a season. The Nations Cup was established in 1967. (See *World Cup.*)

Night skiing — skiing after dark made possible by bright lights on the ski slopes.

Nonstop — timed training runs for downhill in which competitors, one after another, make several runs down the course which will be used in the race. Traditionally, the nonstop is held the day before the competition.

Nor-Am Series — a series of amateur races run annually in the United States and Canada.

Nordic combined — a competition which combines cross-country racing and ski jumping. On an advanced level, results are based on a calculation of the time in a 15-kilometer cross-country race and the best two out of three 70-meter jumps.

Nordic norm — a system of manufacturing cross-country boot soles and bindings to the same standard measurements so that different brands may be used interchangeably.

Nordic skiing — cross-country and ski jumping, both of which developed in Scandinavia, are referred to as Nordic disciplines.

Norm point — see *N-point.*

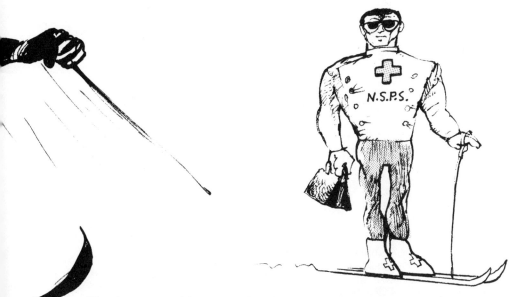

Novice — a skier who has recently begun to learn the sport.

No-wax skis — cross-country skis designed to be used without wax. These generally either have a mohair strip down the center of a fish-scale-type bottom to allow them to glide forward while skiing but prevent them from slipping backward while climbing. Also called "waxless skis". (See *Fishscale*.)

N-point — designation for the norm point of the landing hill below a ski jump where the hill flattens out from the convex knoll to the concave transition.

N.S.P.S. — National Ski Patrol System, the voluntary organization which trains and certifies individuals in rescue, lift evacuation and first aid. (See *Patroller*.)

O

Olympic team — members of a national ski team, such as the U.S. Ski Team, selected to represent their country at the Winter Olympic Games. Three competitors may be entered by each nation in each Alpine and Nordic event; there are also four-member relay teams in cross-country and biathlon competition.

Open gate — a slalom gate in which the two poles are set across the hill, permitting the racer to ski through straight down the fall line.

Outrun — the section at the bottom of the landing hill of a ski jump where the skier slows down and comes to a stop.

P

Pacesetter — a professional skier who competes in a series of races against other pacesetters from across the United States to determine a ranking among them (known as the national standard). Recreational skiers' times are compared to pacesetters' times in NASTAR races. (See *NASTAR*.)

Pacesetting trials — a series of competitions in which professional pacesetters race against one another to determine the ranking among them.

Parallel turn — a turn in which the skis are together throughout the turn, which is initiated with a weight shift, pole plant and use of the edges.

Parka — a warm jacket designed for skiing, usually made of a wind-resistant, moisture-repellent shell lined with down or artifical-fiber fill.

Patroller — a person responsible for controlling safety on the slopes, administering first aid and undertaking rescue activities. Patrollers may be volunteers or paid professionals employed by ski areas. (See*N.S.P.S.*)

Piste — a French term for ski trail which is used all over Europe. In the Alps, *pistes* above the treeline are marked by numbered disks affixed to colored poles that are stuck into the snow.

Plate binding — a binding in which the boot is clamped onto a metal plate which, in turn, is set into a release binding during skiing. (See *Release binding.*)

Platterpull — another name for a *Pomalift.*

Pole — a tube, now usually of lightweight metal equipped with a handgrip, pointed tip and basket which a skier uses to aid in balancing and to pivot around briefly during a turn.

Pole plant — touching the tip of the ski pole into the ski. In Alpine skiing, the pole plant is generally the gentle touch of the pole tip to the snow to help a skier's timing. In cross-country, it is a forceful maneuver in conjunction with the kick portion of the stride.

Poling — using strong arm thrusts to jab both poles into the snow to help propel a skier across flat terrain or in a flat section of a race course in Alpine skiing. In cross-country, poling action is coordinated with each stride.

Pomalift — a lift with discs attached to poles that are suspended from a moving overhead cable, which pulls skiers uphill. The skier stands up, inserts the disc between his or her thighs and is propelled uphill with the skis remaining on the snow.

Pool — a group of ski equipment and clothing manufacturers who have paid a national ski team for the privilege of having top racers use their equipment.

Powder —light, fluffy, new-fallen snow which has not been packed down by machine or by skier traffic.

Prejump — lifting the skis off the snow on the uphill side of a bump to avoid being hurtled off the lip of the bump; used especially in downhill racing.

Profile of the hill — a drawing depicting the cross-section of a hill, including the angle of the slope at all points. Usually describes a jump and its landing hill.

Progression — the sequence of maneuvers taught in ski school according to principles laid down by an organizing group such as the Professional Ski Instructors of America.

Pro racing — racing where competitors vie for prize money. There are professional ski racing tours for both men and women.

P-tex — a synthetic compound applied to the bottom of Alpine skis during manufacturing to protect the running surfaces and help them slide more easily.

P-tex candle — a stick of P-tex which is melted and dripped onto the bottom of a ski to fill in gouges.

R

Race — a competition where the object is to ski faster than all other participants. Style is not a factor in determining the winner of a ski race.

Racing camp — a program established during winter holidays at ski areas or in summer on high-mountain glaciers with special coaching in racing techniques.

Racing helmet — protective headwear consisting of a strong plastic shell which is worn by downhill racers to guard against head injury.

Racing pants — tight-fitting pants made of stretch fabric. Racing pants are often ankle-length and sometimes have a small reinforced "window" at the bottom for the top buckle of the boot.

Racing step turn — a turn in which the racer accelerates or changes his or her line from one gate to another by forcefully pushing off the downhill ski and rapidly shifting weight to the uphill ski, which has been moved up and forward to make the turn.

Racing sweater — a ski sweater with thick padding on the elbows and shoulders designed to protect the skier who bumps against slalom poles while racing.

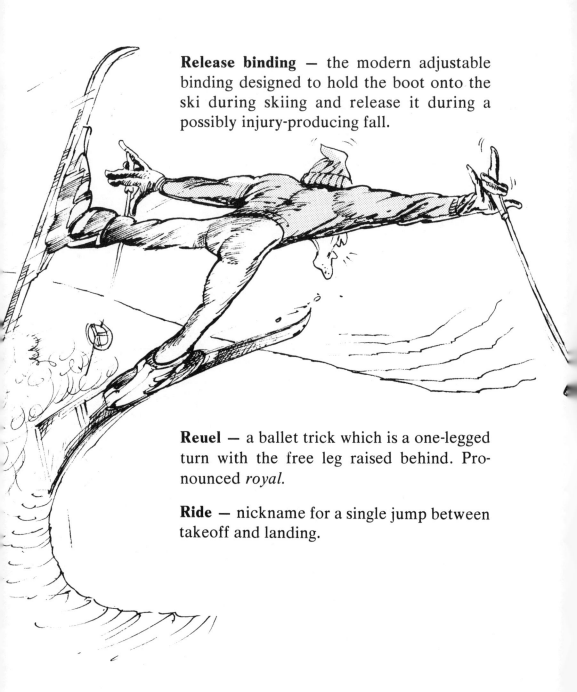

Release binding — the modern adjustable binding designed to hold the boot onto the ski during skiing and release it during a possibly injury-producing fall.

Reuel — a ballet trick which is a one-legged turn with the free leg raised behind. Pronounced *royal.*

Ride — nickname for a single jump between takeoff and landing.

Rope tow — an uphill lift which consists of a continuous loop of rope which skiers grab onto to be pulled up a slope.

Rotation — any turn in which the motion of the body around an imaginary axis is made in the direction of the turn.

R.S. — the abbreviation of *Riesenslalom,* the German word for giant slalom. Skis designed for this type of racing in German-speaking countries are often designated as RS models.

Roch Cup — a long-established and prestigious American downhill race held at Aspen, Colorado.

Ruade — an old-style turn which is accomplished by lifting the tails of both skis off the snow and pivoting around the tips.

Running gates — training for slalom and giant slalom skiing by repeatedly skiing through courses marked by gates, as in a race.

Running surface — bottom of the skis.

Ruts — troughs carved, especially in a slalom or giant slalom course, by the passage of many skiers in exactly the same track.

S

Safety bar — a metal bar which the skier lowers in front of him-or herself while riding uphill on a chairlift. Usually, the safety bar is connected with a footrest which comes up under the chair to provide support for the skis during the ride uphill.

Safety binding — originally, another name for the release binding. Manufacturers discourage the use of this term.

Safety gate — a device at the upper portion of a lift which is tripped to stop the lift if a skier does not unload at the proper place.

Safety strap — a strap of leather or synthetic cord which is snapped onto the boot to prevent the ski from hurtling out of control down the mountain when the binding releases. Safety straps are being replaced by ski brakes. (see *Ski brake.*)

Schuss — pointing the skis straight down the fall line and skiing as quickly as possible without turning or checking. (See *Check, Fall line.*)

Seeding — the practice of ranking skiers for a season's competition based on previous winter's results. In World Cup racing, competitors are seeded by the F.I.S. in groups of 15 in each of the three Alpine disciplines: slalom, giant slalom and downhill.

Shovel — portion of the ski which flares out just before the tip; the widest part of the ski.

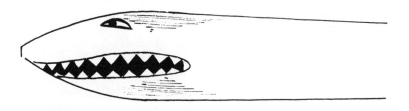

Side camber — an arc built into each side of the ski to help it turn when the skier applies pressure to the edge.

Sideslip — releasing the edges so that the skis drift sideways down the slope.

Side stepping — climbing uphill with the skis perpendicular to the fall line.

"Single!" — a call in the liftline for a double chairlift or T-bar when seeking a riding partner. If a ski area is busy, often it will not allow single riders on the tows.

Sitzmark — an indentation in the snow left by a skier who has fallen.

Skating — skiing on one foot at a time and pushing off with the edge of the free foot to increase speed. Skating is sometimes used by recreational skiers on flat sections but is most often used by racers to pick up speed at the top of a course or near the bottom.

Ski brake — a device held flat and parallel to the ski by the boot which is released at the same time a binding releases to prevent the ski from hurtling out of control down the mountain. When released, the ski brake's two prongs dig into the snow.

Ski bum — a person who takes a job at a ski area in order to be able to ski as often as possible, even if the pay for the job is low.

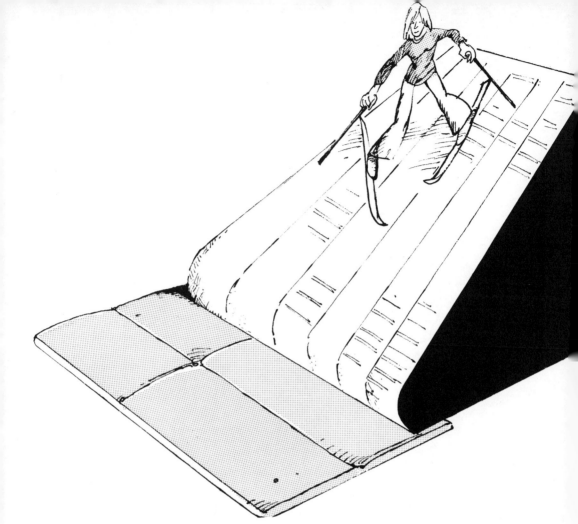

Ski-deck — an artifical slope constructed of a moving, carpet-like material on a continuous band. Ski-decks can be transported on the backs of trucks and are frequently used at ski shows.

Ski foil — a small piece of plastic, often shaped like an A, which is mounted atop the shovel of an Alpine ski to prevent the tips from crossing, especially in slalom racing.

Ski flying — a form of ski jumping on hills where distances of more than 100 meters are reached.

Ski jumping — the sport of gliding down a long ramp and attempting to travel through the air as far as possible before landing. In competition, the score is based on a combination of distance traveled and points awarded by judges for style.

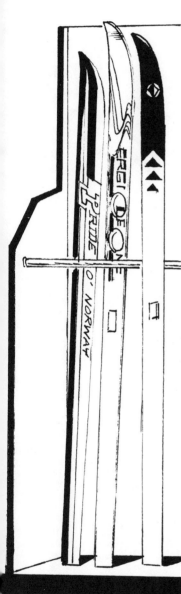

Skimeister — a competition that is a calculation of a skier's performance in four events: cross-country racing, ski jumping, slalom and giant slalom.

Ski mountaineering — a combination of mountain-climbing and cross-country skiing skills used in high-mountain terrain which is not served by lifts and which does not have marked and groomed trails.

Ski-off — the practice of having each skier planning to take a lesson make a few turns so that the ski school supervisor can tell which class would be most suitable for each person.

Ski rack — a device fitted onto the top or trunk lid of a car designed for carrying several pairs of skis. Also, metal or wood stands outside a ski area base lodge against which skiers may rest their skis and poles.

Ski report — ski condition broadcasts on radio or in newspapers giving the amount of snow on the slopes and the type of skiing surface.

Ski school — an organized group of instructors who give lessons at a ski area.

Ski shop — a sporting-goods store specializing in ski equipment and clothing.

Ski stopper — another term for *ski brake*.

Ski touring — another name for recreational cross-country skiing.

Ski tuning — repairing the bottoms; filing the edges and waxing Alpine skis.

Ski week — a five- or seven-day ski vacation, usually including ski lessons every day.

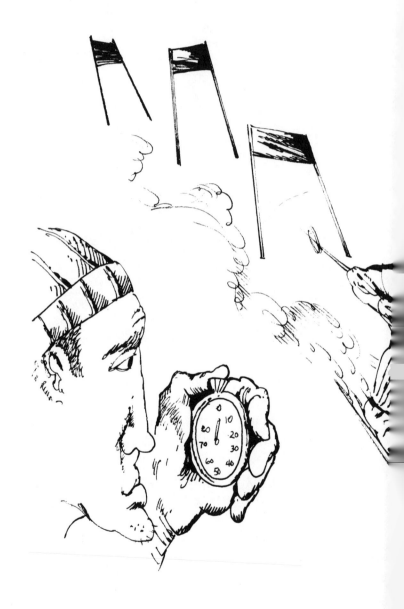

Slalom — the discipline of Alpine ski racing which requires two runs down a short, steep course set with many gates. Two runs are made and the results are based on the combined time. In World Cup racing, men's courses contain 55-75 gates and women's contain 40-60 gates.

Slalom pole — a lightweight, flexible pole stuck into the snow to mark the gates of a racing course. Patrollers often use slalom poles to mark hazards on the slope.

Slope — term used to describe a hill's downward pitch. Also, ski terrain that is wider than a trail.

Snowcat — a large tractorlike machine which is capable of climbing up and down steep hills. It is used for snow grooming, over-snow transport and sometimes rescue operations.

Snow gun — a device which sprays compressed air and water to produce machine-made snow.

Snowmaking — the technology of producing snow by machinery that mixes compressed air and water. Machine-made snow is not a crystal like natural snow but a small, lightly frozen pellet of water that provides a denser skiing surface than natural snow.

Snowplow — a maneuver used to control speed or come to a stop in which the tips of the skis are pointed toward one another and the tails are thrust out to each side. Now frequently called the "wedge."

Snowplow turn — a basic beginner's turn in which the tips of the skis are pointed toward one another, the tails are thrust out to each side and the turn is made by shifting the body weight slightly in the opposite direction from the intended turn. For example, to turn left, the skiers shifts the body weight onto the right ski. This is also called "steering."

Spoiler — a high, rigid support inserted into the back of a ski boot and extending behind the calf which allows the skier to sit back on his or her skis.

Spread eagle — an upright aerial maneuver in which the skier spreads one ski out in each direction while in the air. When the skier opens his or her legs, closes them and opens them again before closing them for the landing, it is known as a double spread eagle.

Spring Series — a series of races run in the United States after the conclusion of the World Cup which gives up-and-coming young amateurs the opportunity to race with established skiers.

Starting gate — a slight rise on the top of an Alpine race course which contains electronic timing equipment and is under the supervision of a race official called the starter.

Steering — moving and weighting a ski to inaugurate a turn. This is used primarily by beginning skiers in a snowplow or wedge turn.

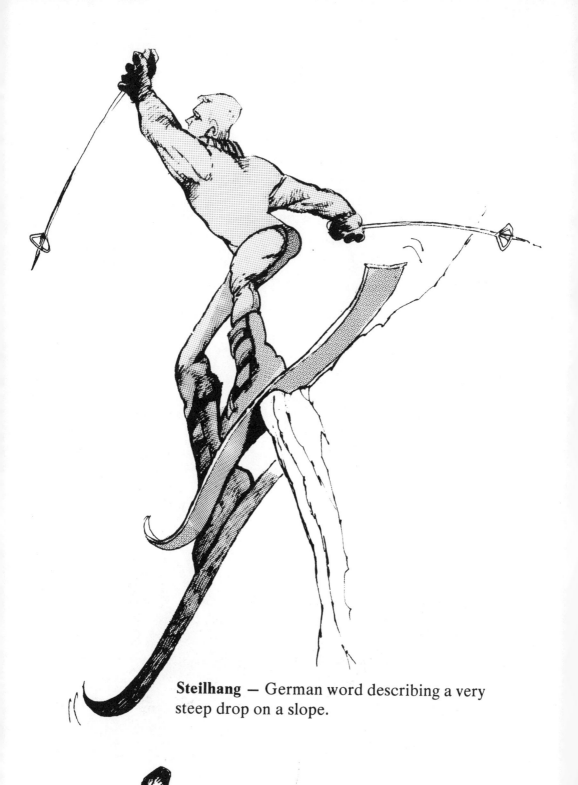

Steilhang — German word describing a very steep drop on a slope.

Stem — picking up the tail of one ski and moving it off to the side while keeping the tips together.

Stem christie — a turn which is initiated by picking up the tail of the outside ski, moving it to the side so that the skis form a V position and shifting the weight to that ski. In the middle of the turn, the two skis are brought parallel together, and the turn is completed with a sliding motion.

Stem turn — a turn which is initiated by picking up the tail of the outside ski, moving it off to the side so that the skis form a V position and shifting the weight to that ski. This motion will cause the turn. When the turn has been completed, the new inside ski is picked up and moved back parallel to the outside ski.

Step-in binding — a release binding which snaps shut when the skier steps his or her boot into the heelpiece.

Step turn — a method of turning around while standing in one spot, done by moving one ski after the other around in a circle. This can only be done on a fairly flat place.

Stick — British term for ski pole.

Surface lift — a lift which a skier rides while standing up on his or her skis to be pulled or propelled up a hill. Surface lifts include J-bars, T-bars and Pomalifts.

T

Tail protector — a small metal piece affixed to the tail of a ski.

T-bar — a lift with which skiers are pulled uphill by a series of T-shaped poles suspended from a moving overhead cable. Two skiers at a time may ride on each "T." The skiers stand up and are propelled uphill by half of the "T" behind their thighs with the skis remaining on the snow.

Téléférique — French word for tram.

101

Telemark — a turn started by pushing one ski ahead of the other at an angle. The skier puts his or her weight on the leading ski and bends the back knee deeply. When the turn has been completed, the back knee is straightened and the skis are brought together. The telemark is used in deep snow and has become popular with expert cross-country skiers. Ski jumpers land in a telemark stance without turning.

Tenth Mountain Division — the ski and mountaineering troops trained by the U.S. Army during World War II, many of whose veterans went on to become pioneers in the postwar ski industry.

Terrain garden — an area set aside for ski instruction of very small children, with bumps built into the snow and cut-out wooden figures set up for children to ski under and around.

Three-sixty — a 360-degree, full-rotation aerial freestyle maneuver.

Tip — the foremost portion of the ski, which is turned up so that it does not dig into the snow.

Tip drag — a ballet trick in which the skier skis on one foot while dragging the tip of the free ski behind and to the side while turning.

Tip drop — an upright aerial freestyle maneuver in which the skier points the tips of both skis down while in the air.

Tip protector — a small metal piece affixed to the tip of a ski.

Tip roll — a trick in ballet skiing in which the skier, aided by a firm pole plant, makes a full body rotation by pivoting over the tips of both skis.

Toepiece — the portion of a binding which holds the toe of the boot to the ski.

Torsion — a ski's ability to resist twisting along its length.

Track — a path taken by a skier, especially through soft snow. Also, a groove made on a cross-country course for skiers to follow.

Trail — a term used to describe a marked ski run. It can either be an Alpine slope, cut through the woods, a route marked down a wider open slope, or in ski touring, a route packed down with sets of tracks for skiers to follow.

Trail map — a drawing, generally printed in a brochure given to skiers, which shows the layout of a ski area's terrain, lifts and buildings.

Trail marking — a series of standard symbols used to describe the relative degree of difficulty at a ski area. In the United States, a trail marked with a green circle is among the easiest slopes. One marked with a blue square is ranked as more difficult and one marked with a black diamond is among an area's most difficult. Skiers often erroneously interpret these signs as standing for slopes designed for skiers of novice, intermediate or expert ability. This is not so. Trail marking is designed to compare each trail to all others at an individual area rather than describe the degree of skill required to ski each slope.

Tram — an aerial lift consisting of two balanced cars carrying a large number of skiers (up to 120 per car). One car goes up while the other comes down. Skiers take off their skis and hold them. Riders stand up in the cabins. Also called "aerial tramway."

Transition — a relatively flat section between two steeper portions of a race course. Also, the section of the landing hill below a ski jump where the angle begins to change from the downward slope to the level area of the outrun.

Traverse — to ski across the fall line of a slope.

Tricks — another name for ballet skiing maneuvers in freestyle.

Tuck — a position assumed in the straight sections of a downhill course for maximum speed and minimum wind resistance. The racer spreads the skis in a fairly wide, stable position and hunches down over the skis. The back is parallel to the snow and the arms are carried as close to the body as possible.

Turtleneck — a long-sleeved, high-collar pullover worn over longjohns and under a ski sweater.

Two-wax system — a simplified selection of two basic cross-country waxes, one for use when the temperature is above freezing and the other when it is below.

U

Unweighting — the act of briefly releasing the body weight from the skis in order to help start a turn. To up-unweight, the skier rises briefly from bent knees. To down-unweight, the skier quickly sinks from a bent-knee position into a deeper knee bend.

Uphill capacity — the maximum total number of skiers who can be conveyed uphill if every place on the lift is filled. Uphill capacity is usually measured in number of skiers per hour.

Uphill christie — a basic parallel turn in which the skis remain parallel while the body weight shifts so that a turn across the fall line is initiated.

Uphill ski — in a traverse, the ski which is higher on the slope.

Upright aerials — maneuvers in freestyle skiing in which the skier does not perform any flips but does tricks involving changes of foot positions.

U.S.S.A. — United States Ski Association, the amateur skiing organization of America, whose activities include sanctioning local and regional ski competition.

U.S.S.E.F. — U.S. Ski Educational Foundation, the organization which raises money and runs the U.S. Ski Team.

U.S. Ski Team — the team which represents the United States in major international Alpine and Nordic ski competitions. These skiers are divided, in most years, into the A-Team, B-Team, C-Team and Development Team.

V

Vasaloppet — a 52-mile cross-country marathon run annually in Sweden, that attracts 10,000 participants. It is regarded as the world's most popular distance race.

Vertical drop — the difference in altitude between a ski area's uppermost lift unloading area and the bottom of the skiable terrain. In the United States, vertical drop is measured in feet; elsewhere it is measured in meters.

Verticle rise — the difference in altitude between a ski lift's loading area at the bottom and unloading area at the top.

Waist — the narrowest part of the ski, where the binding is mounted.

Wand — a short, straight rod which is positioned in front of the racer's knees at the start of a slalom, giant slalom or downhill race. At the "go" command, the skier pushes off from the starting gate and moves the rod which activates the electronic timing system.

Wax — a substance applied to the running surface of a ski. For Alpine skiing, wax reduces friction and affords the skier increased control.

For cross-country skiing, wax allows a ski to slide forward but restrains it from sliding backward. It does this by allowing the

113

ski to glide when it is in motion but gripping the snow when the ski is set down and weighted. Waxes of different colors are keyed to different temperatures and snow conditions both for Alpine and Nordic skiing.

Wax of the day — the wax appropriate for the day's weather and snow conditions.

Wedeln — pronounced *vaydeln,* a series of short, quick parallel turns straight down the fall line characterized by the swing of the ski tails from one side to the other.

Wedge — a maneuver to control speed or come to a stop in which the tips of the skis are pointed toward one another and the tails are thrust out to each side. The traditional name is "snowplow."

Wedge christie — a turn which is initiated by pushing the tails of the skis into a wedge or snowplow position. As the skier crosses the fall line, weight is transferred to the outside ski. The inside ski is then brought next to it, and the turn is completed with the skis parallel.

Wheelie — a trick turn, often done over the top of a mogul, in which the skier has his or

her weight far back on the tails of the skis and
assumes a deep sitting position.

Whiteout — a condition of extreme fog on snow in which it is difficult (or impossible) to differentiate the snow and the sky. High in the mountains, being in a whiteout is actually being in a cloud.

Wide-track-turn — a style of skiing, especially for beginners, in which the skies are kept comfortably far apart to provide stability while learning a turn.

Windpack — snow which has been packed down by the wind, often with a rippled, wavy surface.

Windshirt — a light, unlined jacket of wind-resistant fabric designed to be worn as an extra layer on cold days or with just a sweater on warm days.

Wipe out — to fall.

Wooden skis — for decades, only skis whose main structural element were wood existed. In the 1950s, metal skis were developed for Alpine skiing. A decade later, fiberglass skis became popular first for Alpine skiing and later for Nordic skiing. Some cross-country skis, however, are still made of lightweight wood.

World Championships — Alpine and Nordic World Championships are held under F.I.S. regulations in non-Olympic, even-numbered years. The F.I.S. considers Olympic events to be world championships as well and awards medals to the top three place-winners in each ski competition. There are no world championship-level ski meets in odd-numbered years. (See *F.I.S.*)

World Cup — a trophy given for the best overall performance in the winterlong series of international races in which only the elite men and women may compete. Top placings in each competition are assigned specified numbers of points and, at the end of the season, the leader is awarded a large crystal trophy. The Alpine World Cup was founded in 1967; the Nordic World Cup was begun in 1979.

World Pro Skiing — name of the leading men's professional racing circuit.

Z

Ziel — German word for "finish," which is often seen written on a large banner over the finish area at European ski races.

Zielschuss — German word describing the final section of a downhill course from the final control gate to the finish line (or *ziel.)*